TIMING YOUR INVESTMENTS

A reader, who uses any of the concepts or formulas developed in this book, does so, at their own risk.

The book was written in such detail that a reader can manually duplicate the formulas and spreadsheets documented in this book. The spreadsheets are written in Excel 2007.

NOTE: The chart service mentioned in the text of this book is Worden Brothers TC-2000 ®.

INTRODUCTION

There is no doubt, that confidence is required, when investing significant amounts of money. Consequently an investor must select an investment concept that aligns with their investment philosophy. I make no judgment as to which investment concept is a superior method of investing.

My concept of investing is, "Whatever works." Therefore, this belief has led me to pursue various investments.

When investing in the 2010 to 2013 time frame, it may be difficult for some to believe that at times, fixed income investments are an optimum investment. Also, in this time frame, it should be vividly evident to a fixed income investor, that to maximize their return, they should carefully pursue other investment concepts.

My view of investing has required me to determine which investment is optimum for the current economic situation. Beyond a doubt, this concept is challenging. That has not deterred me from pursuing this method of investing.

Since we live in a dynamic world, the procedure to select an optimum investment is not a static procedure. Periodic adjustments to the procedure may be required. This will be discussed in this book. Also, this concept does not preclude holding certain investments for a number of years. This book details the procedure I am currently using.

TABLE   OF   CONTENTS

Where should I invest my money?

CHAPTER 1

OVERALL INVESTMENT STRATEGY

What I present in this book is what I have assimilated from almost fifty years of investing. I reluctantly use the terms "asset allocation" and "market timing" for I am not sure who sets the standard for their definitions. I read an article in which the author described asset allocation, where his current allocation, was the selection of different stocks. I have no issue with this, as long as one selects stocks that can weather turbulence. My only concern is that it requires a great deal of faith. To me asset allocation means using a broad selection of investments; stock market and non-stock market investments, as the current investments. If the conditions are favorable I feel that fixed income investments can be an optimum investment.

Although it is analogous to walking the high wire, selecting optimum investments, could lead to the highest return. To me investing is similar to Aesop's fable about the "Tortoise and the Hare". For investment purposes, my only change to the fable is that during the race, at times, I invest in the Hare, and at other times I invest in the Tortoise. I don't know whether the "non timing investors" have used all the concepts that are presented in this tome. The concepts presented in this tome have served me well.

That said I present the following.

Money that you do not need for your daily needs has value. If you buy a safe and put your excess cash into the safe, over time, you are losing money. You are losing the return you could earn from the money and secondly, you **may** have a loss in buying power due to inflation.

Investment success is correlated with optimizing the **Time Value of Money**. What I mean by **Time Value of Money**, is the length of time it takes an investment to increase in value. Is your money going to increase in value in one day or six years? To this investor, it makes good common sense, to move your money to the investment that provides an optimum return and the minimum risk. Consequently, to maximize return, an investor should have expertise in multiple investment candidates and temporally blend them, such that, a combined maximum return is obtained. I feel that with **all** investments, timing is important. This was vividly evident with real estate, during the 2002 to 2009 time frame. That is the reason this book encourages an investor to consider investing in various investments. **Temporally blending your investments is no easy task, but I feel that you cannot succeed if you do not try**. This requires an investor to assess the current economic situation.

The allure of the stock market is that, at times, an investor can quickly increase their net worth. Simply stated, with a major upward move in the stock market, one does not have to be very bright to make money in the stock market. Conversely, when the stock market is declining, a great deal of money can be lost in a **shorter** period of time. During these declining periods, being out of the stock market is very comforting. This brings up the often discussed question as to whether to "buy and hold" or attempt to time your stock market investments. Your action will depend on the stocks you are investing in. One can "Buy and Hold," one can trade stocks, or one can do **both**.

There is no doubt, that some buy and hold stocks, will weather market turbulence. An investor must stay in tune with their tolerance of risk. In the following examples, I hope that my attempt at levity doesn't detract from the message.

Let us assume for the moment that Clem Cool, who is worth 100 Zillion dollars, buys some buy and hold stocks and his philosophy is to buy and never sell. Assume that during the holding period, the stock's decline. Clem's net worth drops to 40 Zillion dollars and when asked, "He says oh well." He continues walking and after a long pause he says," They will come back." He then, continues walking and eating his candy bar.

Now, nervous Marti, who earned his money carry bricks up a shaky ladder, buys the same stocks. When they begin to decline in value, he frets, and after some sleepless nights, he decides to sell the stocks. He then watches the stocks closely, and buys them back, when he feels the turbulence has subsided.

I believe that the "buy and hold" concept of investing in some stocks is too stressful for most investors. Why buy and hold and take antacids during severe market declines. Some companies may not recover for years or not recover at all. During a stock market down turn even strong companies, such as the DOW companies, decline. With financially strong companies; they will likely recover. With other companies, if possible, an investor should be in the stock market when the profit potential is the greatest and during declines, wait in other investments for more favorable stock market conditions. The dynamics of some companies is significant. A market downturn that I still vividly remember is the down turn in 1974. Others are 1987, 2000, and 2007-2009.

To maximize your return an investor should gain proficiency in multiple investments. In the author's opinion, during a market downturn, going to cash or zero return, is better than the 56.77% loss, which was realized by the S&P 500 between 2007 and 2009.

In the 2010 to 2013 time frame interest rates available from Money Markets is a modest 0.01%. For those seeking income, dividend paying stocks surely will yield more than a Money Market. In this time frame many of these stocks are slightly over valued.

What's more, in the 2010 to 2013 time frame for those wanting to hold some cash, Banks are definitely a viable alternative to some investment firms Money Markets. In 1981, a thirty year Treasury Security had a **yield of 15.21%**. If the same economic conditions ever return, this investment should be considered as a viable alternative to the stock market. The previous comments vividly highlight that proficiency should be attained in a number of investments.

Over the years, I have had numerous conversations with various investors. It is interesting to note, that none of the people I have talk to, invests in the same manner. As one would expect, people invest in a fashion that aligns with their personal motivation and tolerance of risk. Also, individual investors are a stubborn group. A novice investor should study the various investment concepts and develop their own style. Why pursue an investment concept if you feel uncomfortable with the concept. Find your comfort zone. As an example, you may decide to invest in real-estate. If you have little money, your first real estate investment would probably have to be a "fix up." If you are not the "hammer and nail" type, you may find real estate investing unappealing. If buying and selling options seems too complicated, don't invest in options.

At one time, I had nearly all of my money in CD's and Treasury Notes, yielding what I thought, was a high rate of return. In the fall of 1981, I got interested in the stock market again and started to buy individual shares of stock. The problem was I had hardly any liquid assets. My stock buying was limited by access to my own money. Early withdrawal from my CD's would cause a loss. To enable me to continue to buy stock, I took a loan on the CD's, and also margined the stock I had purchased. Ironically, I was losing money on my stock investments. I still remember being ribbed by a friend about my losing position in the stock market. My comment was, "I'll wait a few years to double my money." It didn't take long to recoup my losses and commence to make money. The beginning of a major bull market was only months away. Loans and margined stock is not a desirable way to invest, since it requires a capital gain from the speculative investments just to break even. With a sizeable stock market gain, this may not be an issue.

To avoid the above-described situation, an investor should maintain a liquid investment to provide money for speculative ventures. This central investment can be thought of as an idling point for your money. The idling investment should have no principal at risk and still have liquidity to enable one to venture out into concepts that hopefully will provide a higher rate of return. There is no point in buying a speculative investment if the resultant after tax return is the same as what can be obtained from a risk free investment.

An investor has to be looking for situations that project to provide a higher rate of return. After an investment is made, the investor should also have a method of evaluating each of his or her holdings, to assess whether to continue to hold that investment. You do not always have to be invested in an investment where capital is at risk. Some investors can only make money in a rising stock market. If you are considering making an investment in real estate and the price of available properties is high, wait for a more favorable opportunity. An investor, who doubles his or her money in a short period of time, can wait safely in an idling investment, until another favorable speculative investment is found. You will still, on the average, have a higher rate of return by just leaving the money in the idling investment. As one gains proficiency in the various speculative investments, money can be moved back and forth from the idle investment, to investment concepts that hopefully provide a higher rate of return.

The above plan sets the whole mathematical process, in that; speculative investments can be compared to the idling investment. If the rate of return from a speculative investment is expected to be greater, venture out from this central idling investment.

I have mainly used money markets available at investment firms as my idling investment. When the after tax return was higher, I have switched to Bank pass books or money markets. At times you may have a considerable amount of money in your idling investment. You should continually monitor the interest rates to assure you are maximizing your after tax return. I monitor interest rates weekly.

It is important to have a time frame in mind for an investment to meet your goals. How many years is a practical limit to hold a speculative investment? The investment has to have a return greater than the return from your idling investment. To assess this, two formula were developed. The amount from a bond investment A_b and the amount from a stock investment A_s versus years of investment.

$$A_b = p_o(1 + i)^n$$

$$A_s = p_o + (p_n - p_{o)})$$

Where n is the number of years invested, p_o is the amount invested, and p_n is the stock price after n years. The following assumptions will be made. The bond price will increase at a simple interest rate of six percent. Stock 1 will pay no dividend and increase in price by one and one half to one. Stock 2 will pay no dividend and increase in price by two to one. With stock 1, which rose in price one and one half times, you can wait seven years and still break even. With stock 2, which rose in price two times, you can wait over twelve years and still break even. **As one would expect, the lower the available bond interest rate and the greater the stock price appreciation, the longer one can wait for the stock price to meet your goals.** This is one reason why low interest rates are good for stock market investments. When you sell a stock, because you got impatient and find that its price has increased by fifty percent one year later, think of the above calculation.

Whether a major portion of your money is invested in speculative investments, depends on your economic outlook. During periods of indecision the idling investment is not a bad place to invest your money; at least you are not losing principal. The portion of your assets that you put into each investment will depend on the experience that you have with that investment type. How much of your assets should you put into a particular investment? The dollar amount is determined by what is prudent for you. What percent of your net worth are you willing to put at risk? One has to strike a balance between experience and investing significant amounts of money. A point to consider is that you are not going to get rich risking small amounts of money. If you invest a dollar and double it, you have two dollars; great. Be assured, if you are not afraid, you are not risking much of your money. The amount is not the issue, it is the percent of your net worth that causes you distress. If the risk causes you distress, you may not be able to make objective decisions. Also, if you cannot sleep nights due to concern about an investment, the added return is hardly worth the grief. It is an individual issue that only you can answer. You have to decide if you have ice water in your veins or whether you are the nervous type. I class myself as the nervous type. I have never, used an idiom of the day, **"gone all in"** in any speculative investment. It's not in my nature. I believe an investor should stay in tune with his or her inner feelings.

Learning to how to invest is similar to learning how to play cards. One can play penny-ante poker and feel that they are a poker player. You probably aren't, but it is a good way to start playing poker. I have never had a reverence for the words "Investment Portfolio." To me, many of the analogous concepts used in gambling, apply to investing. When you are playing with your money, be conservative. When you are playing with the houses money, the bets become just chips and you can become more flamboyant. If you are good at investing, as the years go by, you are continually playing with chips.

As you continue studying investing, you will find that a successful investment plan will include investments that keep you equal and preferably ahead of inflation. These investments will have principle at risk and should be used cautiously.

At the outset, an investor should fully comprehend what they are attempting to do. To be a successful investor you must predict the future. When you buy a stock long, you are predicting that the stock price will rise. When you short a stock, you are predicting that the stock price will fall. If you buy a five-year certificate of deposit, you are predicting that the return you are getting from the CD is going to be higher than your idling investment for five years. No matter what action you take, relative to rare vases, stocks, bonds, or real estate, you are expecting a particular out-come. If you decide to invest on your own, it is your turn to try to predict the future. Unfortunately, if you invest on your own, you will not have the emotional crutch to say, "**THEY** didn't tell me I could lose my money." The success or failure belongs to the person you see when you look in the mirror. To me, this is better than hoping to find a champion for my personal wealth.

Even though I attempt to predict the future, I try to keep it all in perspective; nobody can accurately and consistently predict the future. That is why I studied economic data and developed indicators to attempt to predict a likely direction of the economy. You can make money in the stock market; the challenge is to keep it. For every investment concept there is a season. In one decade the greatest returns, may come from investments in oil and commodities. In another decade the greatest return may come from bonds, stocks and treasury securities. When is it a good time to select a particular investment? This is the challenge an investor is faced with.

To cushion the affect when you are wrong you can use partial purchases or sales. Candidate investments should be compared to one another to develop a sense of the risk versus the reward offered by each investment. Then the investment that offers the greatest return pursued. If no candidates are located, keep your money in the idling investment; at least you are not loosing principal.

Two important considerations are market timing and investment evaluation. Why not invest in a particular investment when the potential for gain is the greatest. Buy low and sell high is a simple statement for success, quite often, a difficult thing to do. People have a strong desire to belong and it takes an iron will to buy when things look bleak and to sell when everybody is buying.

Investment themes must be developed, to locate investment candidates. It should have been apparent, that the tax law change in 1986 would surely slow the speculation in real estate. The more recent real estate excesses of the 2002 to 2007 time frame which was fueled by lending practices and low interest rates, was a disaster waiting to happen.

Hopefully you can find stocks that have continual sales and earnings growth. With these stocks very little effort is required, buy them and don't sell them.

If you want to capitalize on stocks that have wide price fluctuations, you must be aware of the cause of their price variation. With a free market, prices reach an equilibrium modulated by supply and demand. Supply and demand has an effect on most every sought after item, be it computers or pet rocks. When the balance is upset, forces start to react to return the price to equilibrium or establish a new level of equilibrium.

Determining what factors affect a particular investment is paramount to investment success. The factors are not the same for each investment. Each investment concept has its basic factors that do not change. Since investing is a current activity, the factors can change with tax laws, trade agreements and many diverse reasons. The goal is to develop strategies for each investment.

Unfortunately there are times when the price of a commodity is affected by other forces. A story on TV was a situation, which one can only hope doesn't happen too often. In the 2007 time frame, oil began a frighten rise. A TV story alleged that two brokerage houses which also owned oil storage facilities were manipulating the price of oil. The story was not timely; the story surfaced well after the price of oil was well below its high.

The approach!

CHAPTER 2.0

DISCUSSION OF THE APPROACH

I am not selling municipal bonds, stock mutual funds, or whatever. Since I am an octogenarian and I am in a defensive mode. My old investment philosophy, **whatever works**, has required me to study various investments. The next obvious question is what investment is optimum for the current economic state of affairs. This has led me to investigate methods to determine this.

At one time I was able to accurately predict a stock market meltdown. I selected a date of the stock market crash and surprisingly I was within one business day of the event. In chapter 5, I state that I accomplished this. Only a self absorbed fool thinks that they can consistently do this. I developed a spreadsheet program with eleven indicator sheets. In each indicator sheet, I entered data and then analyzed the data. As more indicators indicated, I concluded that the stock market was in peril. Later I added technical analysis.

Currently, I feel to be a successful investor you only have to predict that something is highly probable. I feel that indicators are a notification to **be prepared**. Again, an investor does not need to predict the exact date.

Aside from indicators and technical analysis, to evaluate the investing environment, I also use graphic interpretation of data. When I have felt that the stock market investing environment was not favorable; I have adjusted my investments and in essence, waited for the event. Even though the stock market is surging I have slowly removed money from the stock market and moved most of my capital to investment firm's money markets, or treasury securities. The reason is that, **money is the wood to use when the fire starts again**.

As an example, at one point, I owned stock in 107 individual companies. At the beginning of the slow down, I only owned stock in 11 companies. During the slow down I bought stock in one highly rated company; so at that point in time, I owned stock in twelve companies.

That said I present my approach.

To remain current an investor must adjust.

CHAPTER 3

COMMENTS ABOUT THE ECONOMY

Chapter 3 can be thought of as the procedure transition chapter. The economy went from a period of a housing boom, to a housing meltdown, eventually a stock market crash, and in 2011 to 2013 to a period of "**apparently high money supply.**" The term, "**apparently high money supply,**" beyond a doubt, requires further discussion. This will be discussed later in this chapter.

The concept from 2007 thru the 2009 crash will be discussed first. Then the changes to the procedure for 2013 and beyond will be presented. Chapter 5 contains current indicators, some have been modified, and some new indicators added.

ANALYSIS OF THE STOCK MARKET YEARS 2007 TO 2009

The following is a test of the procedure during a recent market down turn. The recent stock market meltdown; occurred between the years 2007 to 2009. From January 2007 to October of 2007 the score varied between three and five. Indicators, **PPI-A, COMM. MM, Gold,** and **Housing** were the first to indicate a problem. In November of 2007 the score jumped to six in when **Oil** was added to the group; **COMM** dropped out and the **CPI-U** indicated. At this point, included in my technical analysis will be market averages. The SP-500 began to collapse on October 10, 2007. A trend-line drawn from October 10, 2007 to December 13, 2007 was never breached; it was downhill all the way to March 9, 2009, the bottom of the SP-500 during that time period. Chapter 5 defines the indicator symbols.

In February and March of 2008 the score jump to seven when indicators **PPI-A, CPI-U, COMM, MM, Gold, OIL,** and **Housing i**ndicated. From there on the score gradually reduced; by then the stock market was in free fall and stayed well below the trend line to the above mentioned bottom.

The most consistent indicators in driving the market to a bottom were, **PPI-A, MM, Gold, OIL, and HOUSING.** The **CPI-U** stopped indicating a problem in November of 2008. **Housing** began to slow in June of 2007 and was sporadic after that.

The Three Month Treasury Bill **3MTB** only indicated a problem in February & March of 2007. Then again economic conditions did not exist where the **3MTB** would be useful. I still feel that the **3MTB** should be kept as an indicator. There are two reasons it represents a competing investment to the stock market. Also, it is an interest rate that the FED controls.

It seems that since the beginning of time, Gold has been viewed as a safe haven. During periods of inflation, dollar debasement, and uncertainty, investors invest in gold. Almost all of 2006 to 2011 the gold indicator indicated a problem. There were four sporadic months that the gold indicator did not indicate a problem. There was one in December of 2008 and three in early 2009.

GRAPHIC DEPICTION OF MONEY SUPPLY 2006 THRU 2010

I found a graphic depiction of money supply revealing. It is informative, in that, it is readily apparent if money supply is above or below a desired growth rate. An assessment was made for the period from January 2006 thru June 2010.

The money supply graphs I am talking about are the graph of the **percent monthly year over year change in money supply**. I calculated this for both M2 and Divisia M4. I did this because it visibly depicts the changes in money supply. Divisia M4 will be explained in Chapter 5.

The graph has minor wavering. Divisia M4 began to rise and peaked in October of 2008.

In July of 2008 the CPI-U reached a peak of 5.6%.

Divisia M4 began to decrease and in September of 2009 it began to go **negative** and a bottom was reached in June of 2010.

NOTE!! In this discussion of money supply the term **negative** is an analysis term. It really means less money than the same month of the previous year.

In March of 2009 the CPI-U started to go negative and reached a low in July of 2009 of minus 2.1%.

The rate of change in Divisia M4 oscillated and started to rise in February of 2011. There was some wavering as it went positive; but Divisia M4 still appears to be below growth levels.

The graph of M2 has minor wavering. M2 peaked in January of 2009, M2 reduced until March of 2010; it wavered some but did not go **negative**. It then started to rise and peaked in September of 2011 it oscillated narrowly and then its value reduced.

16

CURRENT THOUGHTS ABOUT THE ECONOMY

The FED has been attempting to correct the results of the excesses of the housing boom. To stimulate the economy, encourage employment, and improve the housing market, the FED has kept interest rates low; using what is called Quantitative Easing. They are buying financial assets from commercial banks. This has led some to predict, they are debasing the dollar, and hence this will lead to runaway inflation, higher interest rates, dooms day is near, and a financial meltdown is a possibility. Anything is possible; it depends on the action of Congress, the Administration, the availability of oil, action by the FED, and action by the likely new FED chairman.

From late 2008 to some of 2013, I was able to take advantage of the stock market recovery. The many periods of quantitative easing, has caused low interest rates, this has made it difficult to decide where to invest next. As previously mentioned I am in my mid eighties and near the end of my speculative desires. Occasionally I make a low dollar amount speculative investment. Currently I am in what can be called, an investment holding period; I own some stocks but nowhere near the number I owned in late 2008 and early 2009.

I am not sure that the FED's action will result in runaway inflation. So far inflation seems to be acceptable. Beyond a doubt the author is a layman investor and I am near the limits of my mastery of this subject. Layman investors, don't despair, my knowledge of the subject has served me well. To my knowledge the current economic situation is unprecedented and will probably be studied for years.

I'll provide my thoughts for readers to consider.

1) If the FED prints money and very **neatly** piles the money in a vault in Fort Knox, will this cause inflation? Will this increase the monetary base, debase the dollar, and lead to inflation? Will this limit economic growth?

2) More aligned to what the FED is doing, is to buy financial assets from commercial banks, thus increasing money stored in banks and the monetary base. Why the banks are not loaning the money; tests the limit of my mastery of the subject.

THOUGHTS:

1) Storing money in Fort Knox increases the monetary base but the money is not in circulation. So why would this cause inflation? I don't think it would.

As experienced in the 1930's, not expanding money supply limits the ability of the economy to grow. Money must be available to the business community.

2) In the case of example two, there could well be some restriction limiting the money available to loan. To my knowledge the current situation has not been resolved. As stated above this is where I have no detailed knowledge.

The term "**apparently high money supply**" is a result of the above action. The money supply is high, but so far the money is not in circulation.

3) Is unemployment approaching the FED's target of 6.5 %?

4) Quantitative Easing began in the middle of 2011.

My initial thought was to add an indicator monitoring the reserve requirement; but on second thought I felt that I would monitor the results of their action, by monitoring the PPI-A, CPI-U, Commodities, 3MTB, money supplies, Divisia M4, & M2, gold, oil, housing, and the stock market.

I always felt that unemployment should be included; since the FED has mentioned a value that will cause them to change easing, I added unemployment as an indicator.

ADDITIONAL INDICATOR

I found a paper* by Professor Steve H. Hanke, very informative. A sentence I found interesting is [there is a roughly two-month lag between changes in the USD/EUR exchange rate and the CPI-U; when we factor in this lag, the correlation strengthens to 0.94.] My interpretation of this is that tracking the USD/EUR exchange rate provides a two month lead indication of a change in the CPI-U. To me this provides an advantageous prediction of a change in the CPI-U. The FED's inflation target for the CPI-U is 2.0 to 2.5%. Consequently, I decided to add the USD/EUR as an indicator. Finally, indicators will be developed in Chapter 5.

* "Hyperinflation? No. Inflation? Yes." GlobeAsia April 2013

CHAPTER 4

ECONOMIC DATA

There is great deal of data, used by the government and industry, to gauge markets and the economy. The following is a review of some of the economic data, I would like to comment why I am addressing this enormous task. The reason is; I would like to use economic data, to derive indicators to guide my investment decisions, these indicators will be developed in chapter 5. To that end, I made many trips to the local Federal Reserve Bank and spent many hours studying books and publications in their library. I got on their mailing list for some of their publications and asked many questions. At times I was able to talk to an Economist.

At one time I received in the mail a great deal of data from the Federal Government. I got data on Money Supply, data from the Department of Labor; the St. Louis FED published comprehensive documents on interest rates. I obtained booklets on the Federal Reserve System called "PURPOSES & FUNCTIONS" and "U.S. Monetary Policy and Financial Markets." Ironically most of the data was mailed to me free of charge. I had many years of historical data. Alas, when my wife and I downsized and moved to an apartment, a great deal of historical data was downsized also. Since lately, I am near the end of my investment career I have not bothered to search for hard copy data sources; I have been using on-line data sources.

An author described investing as a battle. When in a battle, with the hope of providing a successful outcome, I feel an investor should have at their disposal, as many weapons as possible.

In some time frames I have had surprising accuracy in timing my investment decisions. Have I got it right all the time? **NO!!** That has not changed my desire to time my investment decisions. An investor, who has been right just a few times, can make a great deal of money.

The following is a discussion of some economic data.

DATA

INFLATION

Of all the economic data available inflation is the most important, and is widely followed. What occurs to me when I think about inflation is the statement, "Today it cost one wheel barrel full of money; tomorrow it's two." As whimsical as the statement seems, inflation could spell the destruction of a countries economy. Since inflation plays such a dominant role in the stability of our economy, the FED closely monitors it. Consequently, you should determine what level of inflation is acceptable. Years ago, I heard someone define 6 percent inflation as moderate inflation. To verify the validity of the statement, the value should be compared with historical data. It is interesting to note that 6 percent inflation, on the average, is slightly less than the infamous average inflation of the 1970's. Following World War II, 1939 to 1949, the average inflation was five percent and for the years 1949 to 1969, inflation on the average was two percent. How can anyone call 6 percent inflation, moderate inflation? Excluding extenuating circumstances, the FED will surely deem 6 percent as an unacceptable level of inflation. This then indicates that a tight monetary policy is likely.

The survival of a countries business community is based on country to country relative inflation. If the inflation rate of all the other countries in the world is 7% and your countries inflation rate is 5%, over a period of time this is a tremendous advantage for your countries business community. In 25 years a $3.00 product, assuming all other factors are equal, will costs $10.16 in your country and $16.28 in the rest of the world, a sizable business advantage. Low inflation is important for price competition nation to nation.

Low inflation is important to people on fixed incomes. With inflation, their purchasing power is constantly being diluted. If you retire early and want to maintain your buying power, you should inflation proof your investments. To maintain your purchasing power your income must, at a minimum, rise at a rate equal to inflation. If inflation is just 3%, prices may double every 23.5 years.

Inflation is measured by determining the price of a constant market basket of goods and services over time. A measure of inflation is the CPI-U. The core rate of inflation is used to assess the rate of inflation of the less volatile items in the CPI-U. A typical scenario is, the CPI will be published, and someone will say, "If you exclude the price of oil and the recent run up in the price of food, inflation is low."

I have difficulty accepting the core rate of inflation as a viable method of evaluating inflation. I am not an economist and have struggled with this concept. I will supply what I think is the reasoning. The reader should evaluate the comments and come to their own conclusion. I have always felt that raw materials are the key first step to inflation and I class oil as a raw material. Oil money leaves the country, thus providing less money to generate sales for U.S. companies. The consumer may just reduce the purchase of the inflated item, causing the price to drop. Also, as long as prices eventually return to normal, inflation is in check. Alternately, the consumer may then purchase less of other commodities to stay within the constant amount of money they have to spend. The reduced demand then causes the non-inflated items to decline in price. This then leads to the argument that an increase in the price of one commodity will not cause inflation. I still feel oil is more important than the average commodity.

Some define the cause of inflation as when the supply of money exceeds the demand for money. It can also lead one to the conclusion that the FED solely determines inflation.

Putting the two arguments together one can postulate that with a nominal money supply an increase in the price of raw materials will have a depressing effect on the economy and the economy will slow. Alternately if there is too much money available, it is similar to pouring gasoline on a fire and it has the effect of overheating the economy.

Again, the main point is what level of inflation does the FED feel is an acceptable value. **My guess is slightly negative to plus three percent. Of late the FED has a target of 2 percent.**

The reason for the discussion is that key commodities may be indicators of impending inflation and they should be a concern to investors. The price of basic needs such as energy, food, and housing should be monitored. I feel that the "supply - demand theory of money" is correct and an excessive supply of money will cause inflation and an insufficient supply of money will slow the economy.

PRODUCER PRICE INDEX (PPI-A) - The PPI-A measures the average changes in prices received by domestic producers of commodities in all stages of processing. A PPI increase should indicate an impending CPI change and possibly inflation.

CONSUMER PRICE INDEX (CPI-U) - The CPI-U measures the price change of a constant market basket of goods and services over time, from a base year. The CPI-U is used to measure inflation at the consumer level.

RAW MATERIALS OR COMMODITIES - The term raw materials is used, to highlight that raw materials are the first level of costs in the production of a product. There are a number of raw materials and they span the alphabet from A to Z. Data is available for single materials and groups of materials. These materials are usually referred to as commodities. To measure commodity prices, data is published as indices using a base year to compare to. There is the spot price (the current price) and the futures price (the price at some date in the future). More than one source publishes data, one being the Commodity Research Bureau (CRB).

Comments on a few commodities:

OIL - Oil is a widely used raw material. It provides heat, fuels our cars, trains, and ships and is literally woven into the fabric of our society. When oil is discussed an investor should pay attention. I do not know of a more important commodity at this time. With the slowdown in the use of nuclear energy for electrical power, we are left with coal, oil, natural gas, water, wind, and wood. The price of oil has an effect on the economy and a factor to be monitored.

COAL - Coal may someday assume an even more important role due to the fact that the USA has so much of it. At this time, I believe coal is the number one fuel used to generate electricity. Its bulk adds to the complexity of transportation. Pollution is another issue that should be researched similar to the Manhattan Project. Hopefully the pollution problem can be solved. There is talk of clean coal technology; one can only hope that this concept is successful.

NATURAL GAS - Natural gas is less polluting than coal or oil and an important commodity. I recently read an article that stated that a product similar to corn ethanol can be made from natural gas. If viable, this should surely be considered as a source for ethanol. The US has ample supplies of natural gas and its use should be federally mandated.

NUCLEAR ENERGY - Nuclear energy may make a comeback someday. **If we are strangled by the high price of oil, nuclear energy may be reconsidered.** A difficult fact, for some to accept, is that under most conditions, it is less polluting than all of the above sources of energy. **This is an enormous, not in my backyard issue.** It would be wise not to build a nuclear power plant on a geographical fault line.

WOOD & BRUSH - Wood is a renewable resource that should be studied as a source of energy. We are getting the pollution from forest fires every year. It doesn't take much of enlightenment to say, "Why not burn the wood and brush for energy?" Pollution again is an issue; but we are already getting the pollution from the forest fires. The cost of property loss, the effort to extinguish the fires, and the loss of lives should be reason enough to consider addressing this issue.

CORN - Corn has been added to the list. I think corn is a poor selection to reduce the use of gasoline. Corn has so many other uses that an increase in demand will cause a price rise in many other products. A better selection is sugar. Many years ago there was no sugar in the average individual's diet. It was a product used by a very few. If you removed all sugar from the American diet, this would be a good thing. To placate the sugar cane growers, use the sugar cane for ethanol. Assuming a dictatorial role I would select an area of the country that is constantly flooding and use wind power to pump water to another area and grow sugar cane or beets. The effort would create jobs, help the American diet, and reduce our dependence on foreign oil. When one considers the political hurdles; I am sure this idea is fantasy land.

PRECIOUS METALS

Gold as a commodity has manufacturing uses. Due to its high cost; it is undoubtedly used when no other alternative material will do. Its properties make it useful in jewelry and its durability make it a coveted possession. Gold is an economic indicator in that it is thought as a safe haven during turbulent periods. The price of gold, for a number of years, was fixed. In 1971 the price of gold was returned to the free market and the price dynamics has been dramatic. In the 2010 time frame, action by the FED to stimulate the economy has caused a rise in the price of gold. Gold has been thought as inflation hedge. My observation has been that gold is not a forever inflation hedge, but can definitely be an inflation hedge during unstable economic periods.

COMMENT ON DATA SOURCES

As mentioned above the Federal Reserve System published booklets called "PURPOSES & FUNCTIONS" and "U.S. Monetary Policy and Financial Markets." This was my source for much of the following. In some cases the booklets are copied verbatim. I tried to get new versions of these booklets and they are no longer available.

INTEREST RATES

Current interest rates are comprised of long-term rates and short-term rates. Short-term rates include federal funds, one-month commercial paper, and three-month treasury bills. Long-term rates include AAA rated bonds, treasury bonds, and tax-exempt bonds.

PRIME RATE - Is the rate posted by large banks as a base for loans to corporations.

FEDERAL FUNDS - Is the rate for overnight loans among financial institutions. The most sensitive short-term interest rate is the FED FUNDS rate.

TREASURY BILLS - Discount rate for treasury bills traded in the secondary market.

DISCOUNT RATE - Is the interest rate charged by the Federal Reserve banks on loans to depository institutions. The Discount Rate precedes the prime.

REAL INTEREST RATE - The RIR is the interest rate minus inflation. You can readily determine whether an investment is providing a return higher than inflation by calculating the real interest rate.

AAA BOND YIELD - Is the interest rate obtained from AAA rated corporate bonds.

RESERVE REQUIREMENT - All banks must meet reserve requirements set by the Federal Reserve. They hold the reserve in the form of vault cash or deposits at Federal Reserve Banks. The holding of these reserves limits the amount of money available to loan. A change in reserve requirement will affect interest rates. Reducing the reserve requirement makes more money available to loan and lowers interest rates. Increasing the reserve requirement has the opposite effect.

COMMERCIAL PAPER - Is short-term promissory notes issued by finance companies and corporations.

MARGIN REQUIREMENT - The Federal Reserve sets the margin requirement, which determines the amount an investor can borrow to purchase stock. As an example if an investor wants to purchase $10,000.00 worth of stock and the margin requirement is 50%, the investor would have to put up $5,000.00 in cash and could borrow $5,000.00 to finance the purchase. The $5,000.00 in cash is the minimum cash required for the stock purchase. Intuitively one can see that the margin requirement affects stock market activity.

INTEREST RATE DISCUSSION

Interest rates determine the economic activity since the level of interest rates can enter in your decision as to whether you can afford a house, a car, or whatever. The Federal Reserve has the tools to control short-term interest rates. It controls interest rates by the purchase or sale of US government securities, the discount rate, and the reserve requirement. The Federal Open Market Committee (FOMC) via a MANAGER at the New York Federal Reserve Bank executes open market transactions. The action taken by the FED affects the non-borrowed reserves at various member banks. When ease is sought the MANAGER purchases more securities than normal. This has an effect to lower the federal funds rate by making more money available to loan. The MANAGER selling securities has the opposite effect on the federal funds rate.

MONEY SUPPLY

There are various measures of money. They are referred to as M1, M2, and M3 and are defined as follows.

 M1 - M1 is a measure of money and includes currency in circulation, demand deposits, and other checkable accounts at commercial & thrift institutions.

M2 - M2 contains M1 and Money market mutual fund shares, Savings & Money market deposits at all depository institutions, Small denomination time deposits at all depository institutions, overnight RP's issued by commercial banks and overnight Eurodollars held by US residents at overseas branches of US banks.

M3 - M3 contains M2 and large time deposits & term RP's at all depository institutions, Money market mutual funds (institutions only), term Eurodollars held by US residents

MONETARY BASE - The monetary base may be measured as the sum of reserve balances with Federal Reserve Banks, plus service-related balances, plus currency circulating outside the Federal Reserve and the Treasury.

DISCUSSION

Stated simply the FED can do what you and I cannot legally do, print money. Generally the FED will have target money growth rates conditioned by the planned growth in the GDP. There is a desire to have sufficient funds to support the economic activity, but not enough to fuel inflation. One way to stifle economic growth is to not have sufficient money in circulation.

HOUSING STARTS

Housing starts is a count of the housing units started in a particular month. The figures are reported by the U.S. Department of Commerce.

DISCUSSION

Many manufactured items are used in the construction of a house. Clearly the more homes built the greater the business activity. This will eventually be reflected in the earnings of the various corporate suppliers.

GROSS DOMESTIC PRODUCT (GDP)

GDP is a measure of the total value of goods and services produced in a nation during the year.

DISCUSSION

A favorable investment climate is when your countries GDP increase is a result of growth not inflationary factors. In the global business arena, your ability to sell your goods to someone else is determined by, politics, whether you have a desirable product, or a cheaper price. Inflation reduces your competitiveness. An expanding GDP is obviously good for investments. The expansion has to be real not inflationary.

EMPLOYMENT - When you are without a job you know what job creation means. Job creation, at times, is an administration media event, essentially saying. "Look what I did." The benefit is twofold. The more jobs created the more content the electorate and the greater the business activity. An important aspect for global business survival is the quality of the jobs.

UNEMPLOYMENT - The measure of unemployment has an acceptable upper and lower boundary. If it is too high there is on concern about the number of people out of work and if it is too low there is a concern about inflation. The lower value of about 5% is analogous to the four-minute mile. It was humanly impossible to break the four-minute mile until somebody did it. Worrying whether the country will go to ruin with full employment is more acceptable than the Great Depression of the 1930's. The above was written in the 1980's. Unemployment has since dropped to 4.3% and nothing serious happened.

DISCUSSION

The Department of Labor reports data on the number of people unemployed.

TRADE BALANCE - Trade balance is the monetary difference between imports and exports. If I sell you apples worth $200.00 and you sell me pears worth $100.00, I have a plus $100.00 trade balance.

DISCUSSION - A concern is whether the business activity ends up adding to the bottom line of corporate America or overseas. A flag should go up if the trade deficit continues to rise even though interest rates are cut. A rise in US corporate earnings may not occur. The US has not enjoyed a trade surplus in a while. A positive or at least a falling trade deficit is generally a bullish sign. The last time the US had a trade surplus was April 1976.

The fact that we are part of a global economy is more apparent now that we are running a trade imbalance. An investor must be aware of the affect that the currency exchange rate has on their investments. Extreme examples will be used to illustrate a point. Let assume that the US buys all their products abroad. The US wealth flows to other nations. Other nation's banks will have an oversupply of dollars in their vaults. The value of your currency in other countries banks is stated as the **Current Account,** this is a term that economist use to indicate the value.

EXCHANGE RATE - If you have traveled to other countries, you are well aware of exchange rates. Exchange banks at airports change your dollars to local currencies depending on a continually changing rate.

RETAIL SALES - Total amount of sales in all U.S. retail stores during a given period.

AUTO SALES - Total number of domestically made cars and trucks sold during a given period.

DISCUSSION - Sales are a measure of business activity in the respect business areas.

UNIT LABOR COST

UNIT LABOR COST - The cost per unit of product output is called unit labor cost. Unit labor cost is reported on a quarterly basis by the U.S. Department of Labor. It is figured relative to a base year.

Nothing succeeds like plain luck. How often?

CHAPTER 5

INVESTMENT INDICATORS

The economic environment, like the weather, is continually changing; consequently, an investor should have expertise in multiple investment candidates. As required an investor must modify their investment selection according to the prevailing economic situation. The intent of this chapter is to develop indicators to guide an investors investment decisions.

In the year 1987, I had some success with the concepts discussed in this chapter. I had in my shirt pocket a note stating **October 15, 1987** as the date of the stock market crash. I called the date **"Black Thursday."** Never the less I was not correct, the crash occurred on **Monday October 19, 1987.** For this type of work the prediction was fantastic. I was off by one-business day. **Dumb luck, maybe,** but in this chapter I will tell you how I arrived at that date. Fortunately prior to the crash I had sold a number of the stocks in my portfolio. Consequently, I was not financially devastated by the crash. This should stress the importance of economic indicators. If one analyzed indicators during late 1986 and the summer of 1987, it was apparent that a problem was on the horizon. Interest rates gradually rose until the crash. That was one of the indicators that highlighted a problem. During that period the PPI-A went from negative 3.77% in December 1986 to a positive 4.48% in August of 1987. The CPI-U went from a positive 1.13% in December of 1986 to a positive 4.29% in August of 1987. The real interest rate went from a positive 16.39% in July of 1986 to a positive 0.715% in August of 1987. It is interesting to note that the FED started raising interest rates in January of 1987 right up to the crash of October 19, 1987. As mentioned above, the data indicated that a problem was likely. The selection of the date was arbitrary. Two conditions that I felt important were cold weather, and the ides of a month; to me that indicated **October 15, 1987.**

DISCUSSION

The Federal Reserve Board establishes monetary policy after reviewing the economic and financial situation. Their goal is to maintain an orderly business environment. The **interpretation** of economic data is not an exact science, all you have to do to realize this, is to watch a few business oriented TV programs, or read a few financial journals.

There are many diverse opinions. Interest rates, unemployment, and the rate of inflation, money supply, and attitude, usually affect investments. You should try to gauge the Federal Reserve's intent from your own indicators and form an opinion about likely market trends. At times there are interest rate peaks or lows that last for many months. These interest rate variations are what an investor should be sensitive to, when deciding where a major portion of his or her assets should be invested. Why consider risky investments if you can obtain a high percentage return from Treasury Securities. It would be informative to know what the FED is contemplating.

At times, conventional logic has nothing to do with market direction. News that one would normally consider good news has a depressing affect on the markets. What is good news and what is bad news has to be sorted out and properly interpreted.

The importance of commodity prices as an indicator must be reviewed. A simplistic example could be; suppose you like chocolate bars and the price of cacao beans rises causing the price of your favorite candy to rise. What affect does this have on the overall economy? More than likely the above event will just affect candy companies. Let us now assume that the price of oil rises. What affect does this have on the overall economy? As previously mentioned oil is an important commodity. A sustained rise in the price of oil will eventually have an effect on business activity, in that; there is less money available to spend on other items. It can be seen that some commodities should be ranked as to their effect on the business activity. Inflation indexes will **eventually** reflect the inflation affect of commodities. The delay in this affect requires an investor to monitor certain important commodities. The information must be current and not history. If one waited for the affect of the price of oil to manifest itself in the inflation indexes an investor could not take advantage of a stock buying or selling opportunity.

One must continually assess whether an indicator has become obsolete. They say that he or she, who does not learn from history, will have to relive it. This is a valid statement that should not be cast in cement. The pertinent point is, are the situations the same such that historical knowledge can be used.

Prior to developing indicators, you should develop sensitivity as to what to expect from the indicators. In some cases you can start with a word statement of a situation and derive an exact mathematical formula to represent the situation. In other cases the formula may represent a ratio that can be used for comparison to historical data. The main point is to know what the formulas can do for you. In some cases, the formulas will provide only an insight as to the likely outcome.

Also, data should be manipulated to enhance information. Some thought should be given to single valued information and relative information. Relative information, can keep the information timely. As an example, let us assume that you develop a concept that defines what action to take when the Dow Jones Industrial Average reaches 8000 and what action to take when the DJIA drops back to 7000. A few years hence the numbers are meaningless. If the concept is still valid the numbers must be modified.

In the 1970's I thought interest rates would never return to 3% again, they did. In fact in 2009 interest rates have gone below one percent. If one compares interest rates to inflation, the comparison is more meaningful, in that a real rate of return is determined. The comparison has more information when presented in this manner and the value has a better chance of remaining current.

One can compare data to itself in the form of moving averages. Information is obtained by comparing current data with an average of past values of the same data. Whatever average you feel is meaningful can be used, ten, thirty, fifty, or two hundred day moving average.

The mathematical game with interest rates, inflation, and market averages is important. A point to keep in mind is that one should not get caught up in the numbers game. Good plain common sense should temper you judgment. Political reality is an important consideration. As an example, let us assume that a number of banks are in a dreadful financial condition. A solution is to raise taxes and use the money to bail out weak banks. Since it is bad politics to raise taxes, a way to strengthen the banking system is to lower short-term interest rates. A bank can now pay low rates to their investors and use the proceeds to buy safe higher yielding Treasury Securities. The banks can get well on the spread. Neat, isn't it? Bank finances are improved and no new taxes are required. Lower interest rates, in this case, has the same effect as raising taxes. This process disconnects interest rates from the reality of the economic situation. This requires cooperation between the FED and the current administration, I have no idea if this has ever happened, but if I were asked to make a guess, I would bet on the mid 1990's!

In the development of indicators, at the outset, I would like to address what can be called statistical relevance. Another way to present the point would be to contemplate cause and effect. A little story might be helpful to clarify my point. I was having supper with my wife, another couple, and a woman I have known since I was a young boy. The other gentleman owned the country club; in fact, he owned the golf course and country club. The only way you could play golf at the golf course was with his approval. He had the chef running back and forth to assure our meals were to our satisfaction. I bring this all up to highlight that this was a very successful man, the golf course was only a hobby. He stated that he liked to bet on horse racing. He mentioned that when he was winning he didn't change his socks. You might think that this story is not related to statistical relevance, but it is. Simply stated, what in the world does not changing your socks, have to do with winning at horse racing. **Obviously nothing**; consequently horse racing and socks have no statistical relevance. For the stock market, indicators that have been mentioned are; whether women wear their dresses above or below their knees, what league wins the World Series, or what league wins the Super Bowl. ***Finally, an indicator should have relevance to what you are attempting to predict.***

Initially, the only indicator I plotted was the three-month Treasury bill rate, from data I obtained from the Sunday newspaper.

Compared to the sixties, today trends seem to be recognized much faster. Don't be discouraged though, in 2005 I was retired, and I had the highest income I ever had.

A commentator declared that we would have double digit inflation by the end of 1984 using M1, a measure of money supply, as a basis for his analysis. It did not happen. This highlights the danger of using one indicator to determine your economic model.

I have read that the great depression that began in the early 1930's was exacerbated by insufficient money supply.

OVERALL PLAN

To reduce the work load, a multi-sheet spreadsheet program has been developed. The explanation of the overall multi-sheet spreadsheet program is much more complex than the actual process. Once developed, all an investor has to do, is to **monthly** input data for each indicator into a specific data sheet of the multi-sheet spreadsheet program. There will be as many data sheets as there are indicators. In each indicator sheet a calculation will be performed and a score determined. There are two exceptions where multiple calculations are performed on one sheet, they are the market price to earnings ratio and the market dividend yield; the second sheet is where two money supply calculations are made using money supply data. The calculation results from each indicator sheet are automatically inputted into a sheet named **SCORE**. The **SCORE** sheet has fifteen columns, the date column, the sum column, and a column for each of the thirteen indicators. **To assist in interpretation of results, in some indicator**

sheets, in addition to IF statements, graphs of the data will be
generated. I feel that in some cases a graph of the data is more
helpful than just a discrete decision.

Consequently, the approach proposed to gauge the stock market, is to
follow the indicators, analyze the results of the thirteen indicators,
weigh the evidence, and be on alert when three or more indicators
indicate. An investor's concern should heighten as more indicators
indicate. Then I feel it would be wise to assess the stock market
investment environment, as often as time allows, using two methods; in
addition to using the above discussed indicators I would recommend that
an investor periodically assess the stock market direction using
technical analysis and follow the S&P 500, the DJ-30, or whatever
market your stocks are traded in. In addition to the averages an
investor can follow the individual stock that they own. The chart
service has a daily display of the above mentioned averages, and your
stocks, and where they are relative to their moving averages.
Furthermore, an investor can periodically draw trend lines to assess
their direction. At this point an investor should evaluate what the
indicators indicate and attempt to determine the severity of the market
down turn. An investor must now decide whether to hold stocks that are
considered buy and hold stocks and depending on the expected severity
of the market down turn an investor must determine whether to sell
all stocks.

Each individual investor will have to make a decision which aligns
with their financial situation and their ability to endure stress.

DETERMINING INDICATORS

As I mentioned at the beginning of this Chapter, I have had some
success with the concept of indicators. Unfortunately indicators have
a period of regency. An investor must meet head-on any situation and
modify their investment evaluation process accordingly. There are
some new concepts in the measure of money supply. As mentioned in
Chapter 3, due to the large amount of money, in a sense stored, in
commercial banks there is a concern how they loan the money. In the
discussion of each indicator, where warranted; I will comment.

LOCATING INDICATOR DATA

Figure 5-1 contains addresses of the data sites I am currently using.
To provide convenient access, they can be added to your internet
favorite's location.

Another point is the location of historical data. One data source
that I have changed multiple times is the data source for gold. I

finally decided to use a US ETF GLD mainly because current and historical data is readily available from my chart service.

INDICATORS

Inflation is an important indicator to follow. An extreme value undoubtedly is a precursor to the FED taking some action to bring its value to a value that they deem acceptable. I have no insight on the value of deflation that is acceptable; I am going to rely on the control of money supply to indicate the FED's intent in this event.

INDICATOR #1 Percent Change in the Producer Price Index (PPI-A)

DATA SOURCE

Refer to Figure 5-1 indicator number 1.

Inflation will be measured by calculating the percent change of the current months PPI-A value relative to the PPI-A value for same month of the previous year. An increase in inflation will be taken as being bearish and a decrease will be taken as being bullish. The level that is acceptable is less than plus 3%.

Expressed as a formula:

100*((PPI-A this yr.)-(PPI-A last yr,))/(PPI-A last yr.)

The first column (A) in the sheet will contain the month of that year, the second column (B) will contain the value of PPI-A for that month, the third column (C) will contain the above described calculation, and the fourth column (D) contains an IF statement which will be used to determine the score for PPI-A.

IF(G8> 3,1,0)

The score is inputted into the score sheet.

INDICATOR #2 Percent Change in CONSUMER PRICE INDEX (CPI-U)

DATA SOURCE

Refer to Figure 5-1 indicator number 2.

The calculation and comments are identical to those for PPI-A except the data for CPI-U will be used. The level that is acceptable is less than plus 2%.

IF(G8> 2,1,0)

The score is inputted into the score sheet.

INDICATOR #3 USD/EUR Exchange Rate

DATA SOURCE

Refer to Figure 5-1 indicator number 3.

The exchange rate will be used to illustrate that the dollar is being debased. As mentioned in Chapter 3 it is an indication of a change in commodity prices. A graph of USD/EUR will be available in this sheet.

The first column (A) in the sheet will contain the month of that year, the second column (B) will contain the value of USD/EUR rate, the third column (C) will contain the IF statement. If the USD/EUR value is above 1.2 a rise in commodity prices is likely. An investor should then refer to the graph.

$$IF (G8> 1.2, 1, 0)$$

The score is inputted into the score sheet.

INDICATOR #4 – % Change in the price of COMMODITIES (COMM)

DATA SOURCE

Refer to Figure 5-1 indicator number 4.

The calculation and comments are identical to those for PPI-A except the data for industrial commodities is used. The level that is acceptable is less than **5%**.

The IF statement is as follows

$$IF(G8>5,1,0)$$

The score is inputted into the score sheet.

INDICATOR #5 – Value of the THREE-MONTH T-BILL (3MTB)

DATA SOURCE

Refer to Figure 5-1 indicator number 5.

The FED can control short term interest rates by the purchase or sale of Treasury Securities. The level of the Three month Treasury Security presents an alternative investment to the return from speculative investments; hence the level is an indicator. In the past I have used five percent and feel this is still an acceptable value. My logic is that five percent is a yield where I would consider buying a five year Treasury Security. Consequently, a Value of five percent will be used.

The first column (A) in the sheet will contain the month of the year, the second column (B) will contain the value of the Three Month T-Bill for that month, the third column (C) will contain an IF statement which will be used to determine the score for the Three Month T-Bill.

$$IF(G8>=5,1,0)$$

This score is inputted into the score sheet.

MONEY SUPPLY

There are two concerns related to money supply. The first is if there is too much money in circulation, this may cause inflation. The second concern is if there is too little money in circulation this may slow economic activity. It is unlikely that the two indicators will conflict, so they will each have a column in the score sheet.

INDICATOR #6 – MONEY MULTIPLIER (MM)

DATA SOURCE

The seasonally adjusted M2 data is available on-line from the following source:

Refer to Figure 5-1 indicator number 6 (a).

The seasonally adjusted monetary base is available on-line from the following source:

Refer to Figure 5-1 indicator number 6 (b).

NOTE!! Past data is usually updated. To keep the data current; when new data is downloaded; I always review past month's data and update the past months data as required.

I read an article by Professor Steve H. Hanke*, in which he discusses a **money multiplier** as a measure of an inflationary condition. The money multiplier is M2 divided by the monetary base. In his article he states and I quote [When the demand for the more narrowly defined kind of money goes down, as it eventually will, the money multiplier will move back into it normal range of 8 to 9. That is, the dollars manufactured by the FED will give rise to more money (broadly defined) burning holes in people's pockets. An excess of money in spenders' hands is a recipe for inflation.]

* FORBES December 14, 2009

The first column (A) in the sheet will contain the month of the year, the second column (B) will contain the value of M2 for that month, the fourth column (C) will contain the value of the monetary base for that month, [Note all values are seasonally adjusted values], and the fifth column (D) will contain the calculation which is as follows:

$$= 1000*(B5/C5)$$

The 1000 is to make M2 the same dollar units as monetary base. The sixth column contains an IF statement to determine the score of the ratio of M2 to monetary base and is as follows:

$$IF(D4>8,1,0)$$

This score is inputted into the score sheet.

INDICATOR #7 – MONEY SUPPLY MONITOR (MSM)

DATA SOURCE

The seasonally adjusted Divisia M4 data is available from the following source:

Refer to Figure 5-1 indicator number 7.

The follow comments are to clarify why there are two measures of money supply. As previous mentioned the control of money supply is a difficult challenge. As stated above the money multiplier **MM** is a determination of excess of money in circulation. Now the money supply monitor **MSM** will be used as a measure of contraction of money supply. This occurrence took place in the early 1980's, when the FED, with Paul Volker as the FED chairman, vigorously contracted the money supply. The monetary dynamics were startling. **Note!** Divisia M4 was not available in the 1980's

I recently purchased a book by Professor William Barnett entitled "Getting It Wrong"- How Faulty Monetary Statistics Undermine the FED, the Financial Systems, and the Economy. It was published in 2012 by the MIT Press.

In his book, it is proposed that a superior measure of money supply is Divisia M4. Currently a measure of money supply is M2. M2 is a simple sum of components of money. It is proposed that a superior measure of money supply is a weighted sum of the various components of money. With Divisia M4 each component is assigned a weight depending on its usefulness as a medium of exchange; thus providing a superior representation of money supply. All I am taking from Professor William Barnett book is that, Divisia M4 is a superior measure of money supply;

consequently I am using it in my analysis. The following analysis of Divisia M4 data is my own interpretation of the contraction of money supply.

I thought I would comment prior to developing any formulas. To sustain economic growth a positive measured amount of money must be made available. In the nineteen thirties insufficient supply of money stifled economic growth. Indicator **MSM** will measure whether money supply growth is positive.

In this page prior columns are utilized to calculate the money multiplier **MM**. The first column contains the month of the year, the seventh column contains the value of Divisia M4 for that month, the eighth column contain the percent year over year change in Divisia M4, the ninth column contains an IF statement. I do not know the percent planned growth in money supply. If I did I would use it instead of one (1) in the IF statement.

Eighth column formula is as follows:

$$= ((G17/G5)-1)*100$$

Ninth column formula is as follows:

$$IF(H17<=1,1,0)$$

The score is inputted into the score sheet.

GRAPHIC ASSESSMENT OF MONEY SUPPLY

A graphic depiction of money supply can probably be a standalone assessment of money supply. It is informative, in that, it is readily apparent if money supply is above or below a desired growth rate. This is repeated, because I strongly feel it is worth repeating. Also, there is further discussion in Chapter 6.0.

An assessment was made for the period from January 2006 thru June 2013 by plotting the year over year percent change in M2 and Divisia M4 on the same graph.

The money supply graphs I am talking about are the graph of the **percent monthly year over year change in money supply**. I calculated this for both M2 and Divisia M4. I did this because it visibly depicts the changes in money supply.

The graph has minor wavering. Divisia M4 began to rise and peaked in October of 2008.

In July of 2008 the CPI-U reached a peak of 5.6%.

Divisia M4 began to decrease and in September of 2009 it began to go **negative** and a bottom was reached in June of 2010.

NOTE!! In this discussion of money supply, the term **negative** is an analysis term. It really means less money than the same month of the previous year.

In March of 2009 the CPI-U started to go negative and reached a low in July of 2009 of minus 2.1%.

The rate of change in Divisia M4 oscillated and started to rise in February of 2011. There was some wavering as it went positive; but Divisia M4 still appears to be below growth levels.

The graph of M2 has minor wavering. M2 peaked in January of 2009, M2 was reduced until March of 2010; it wavered some but did not go **negative**. It then started to rise and peaked in September of 2011 it oscillated narrowly and then its value reduced.

COMMENT ON DATA SMOOTHING

In some of the following calculations, data smoothing will be used; this will be accomplished in some cases by summing multiple months of data to provide smoothing. It probably is easier explained with numbers representing months; 1 is January, 2 is February and so on. Then perform calculations as indicated below.

INDICATOR #8 – The price of GOLD (GLD)

DATA SOURCE

Refer to Figure 5-1 indicator number 8.

Many feel that gold is an inflation hedge. A rise in the price of gold will be taken as a negative for the stock market. The determination will be as follows. The price of GLD on the last business day of each month, the price of GLD will be imputed in a column. The calculation of GLD values is as follows:

Row 1	(E19+E18+E17)/(E7+E6+E5)
Row 2	(E20+E19+E18)/(E8+E7+E6)
Row n	etc.

A review of the numbers shows that the ratio is the sum of three current month's data, to the ratio of three months of data a year ago. It can be seen that if the price of GLD is decreasing the calculation will be less than one and if the price of GLD is increasing the value will be greater than one.

The first column (A) in the sheet will contain the month end date of that year, the second column (B) will contain the value of GLD on that date, the third column (C) will contain the above formula for that month, to determine the score of the summation column the fourth column (D) will contain an IF statement. The investor should take a rising price of GLD as a general attitude of fear is prevalent in the investing community and a negative for the stock market.

$$IF(C19>=1,1,0)$$

The score is inputted into the score sheet.

INDICATOR #9 - The price of OIL (OIL)

DATA SOURCE

Refer to Figure 5-1 indicator number 9.

A substantial year over year rise in the price of oil will be taken as a negative for the stock market.

The data smoothing of the values will be as follows.

Row 1	$100*[((B18+B17)-(B6+B5))/(B6+B5)]$
Row 2	$100*[((B19+B18)-(B7+B6))/(B7+B6)]$
Row n	etc.

I used the above described concept, which is a decision based on the percent yearly rise in the price of oil, until I thought what if oil increases continually, and stabilized at one thousand dollars a barrel. The oil indicator would cease to indicate. Of course, there would be calamity; but still a meaningful indicator should indicate there is a problem. I then decided that I would include a dollar amount in the indicator in addition to the yearly price rise.

The question the investor is faced with is, what percentage year over year rise in the price of oil, will cause the market to fall. I plotted the monthly price of oil and calculated the year over year percent change in the price of oil and the monthly close of the SP-500. It appears that when the year to year percentage change in the price of oil approached sixty percent the SP-500 began to slowly fall. Also, when the year to year percentage change in the price of oil approached ninety percent, the SP-500 average rapidly fell. If the calculated value is greater than sixty percent; this indicates that the price of oil can cause disruption in the stock market. To provide some leeway I have selected fifty percent as a value for an investor to be on alert. The next point is what price to use as an alert; I selected ninety dollars a barrel. This is an arbitrary selection and can be modified as required.

The first column (A) in the sheet will contain the month of the year, the second column (B) will contain the price of oil for that month, the third column (C) will contain the yearly percentage change in the price of oil as defined by the above formula, the fourth column (D) will contain two IF statements as defined below, the fifth column (E) is the score that will be entered in the score column.

Column D IF(C18>50,1,0)+IF(B18>90,1,0)

The following IF statement is the final decision:

Column E IF(D18>=1,1,0)

The score is inputted into the score sheet.

INDICATOR #10 – HOUSING STARTS (HS)

DATA SOURCE

Refer to Figure 5-1 indicator number 10.

Because of the many products used in the construction of a house; housing starts will surely contribute to the business activity. An increasing number of housing starts will be taken as a positive for the economy and the stock market. A decreasing number of housing starts will be taken as a negative for the economy and the stock market.

    Row 9   (B6+B5+B4)/(B3+B2+B1)
    Row 10   (B7+B6+B5)/(B4+B3+B2)
    Row n   etc.

The first column (A) in the sheet will contain the month of the year, the second column (B) will contain the number of housing starts for that month, the third column (C) will contain the above formula for that month, the fourth column (D) will contain the IF statement for that month. It can be seen that if housing starts are contracting the calculation in column (C) will be less than one and if housing starts are growing the calculation will be greater than one. The score will be determined by an IF statement in column D and is as follows.

IF(C9>1,0,1)

The score is inputted into the score sheet.

THE STOCK MARKET

An investor should know where the stock market is relative to a historic stock market peak. A historic peak can provide an investor with an alert. As a measure of extreme values I have selected the P/E and the dividend yield of the S&P 500 stock market index.

INDICATOR #11 - PRICE TO EARNINGS RATIO (P/E)

DATA SOURCE

Refer to Figure 5-1 indicator number 10.

So many factors enter into the selection of a value of P/E that I would call it a soft indicator. People cling to stocks in periods that can be classed as a "white knuckle" periods. People sometimes wait until something similar to a pressure release on a boiler, when their tolerance for stress is reached, they rush to the exits. I am going to select a price to earnings ratio of 19.

A monthly value of P/E will be entered into the spreadsheet. The first column (A) in the sheet will contain the month of the year, the second column (B) will contain the value of the P/E ratio for each month, the third column (C) will contain an IF statement which will be used to determine the score.

The IF statement will be as follows:

$$IF(D8>=19.0,1,0)$$

The score is inputted into the score sheet.

INDICATOR #12 - Market DIVIDEND YIELD (DIV)

DATA SOURCE

Refer to Figure 5-1 indicator number 12.

The calculation is similar to the discussion for the price to earnings ratio. The only difference is that the value of the dividend yield will be entered in that month's cell. A low stock market yield is regarded as an indication of an overvalued market. The thought process is the same as the value of P/E ratio. I am going to select a dividend yield of 2%.

The market P/E and dividend yield will occupy the same data sheet called MKT.

The first column (A) in the sheet will contain the month of the year, the fourth column (D) is a spacer column, the fifth column (E) will contain the value of the dividend yield as described above for each month, the sixth column (F) will contain an IF statement which will be used to determine the score.

The IF statement will be as follows:

$$IF(E8<=2.0,1,0)$$

The score is inputted into the score sheet.

INDICATOR #13 – UNEMPLOYMENT (UNEMP)

DATA SOURCE

Refer to Figure 5-1 indicator number 13.

I wrote the following on an earlier version.

Another possible indicator is unemployment. I instinctively feel that the level of unemployment has some predictive value. I have a feeling, but no proof, that the FED will be more accommodating when there is high unemployment. As of yet I have not determined, with any confidence, a mathematical procedure to score the monthly values of unemployment.

Of late the FED has indicated that they will continue monetary easing until unemployment reaches of value of 6.5% or less.

The first column (A) in the sheet will contain the month of the year; the second column (B) will contain the percent unemployment. The third column (C) will contain an IF statement which will be used to determine the score.

The IF statement will be as follows:

$$IF(E8<=6.5,1,0)$$

The score is inputted into the score sheet.

THE SCORE SHEET

The **SCORE SHEET** provides a monthly determination of the investment environment. The following is an example of the score cell for row sixteen.

=C16+D16+E16+F16+G16+H16+I16+J16+K16+L16+M16+N16+O16

CONCLUSION

An investor can add to the thirteen indicators as conditions warrant.

Another indicator could be government spending; with the current situation year 2013, I feel it would be ill advised to use this as an indicator.

CATASTROPHIC EVENTS

Due to the diversity and numerous possibilities, it is impossible to offer any guidance of how to deal with catastrophic events. As they unfold, an investor will have to assess the effect of each catastrophic event, on their portfolio. Some past examples are the assassination of President Kennedy, the cold war, the Berlin wall up and down, the invasion of Kuwait, the destruction of the World Trade Center Towers September 11, 2001.

ANALYSIS OF THE STOCK MARKET YEARS 2006 TO 2009 - THIRTEEN INDICATORS

The following is a test of the procedure during a recent market down turn using thirteen indicators. The recent stock market meltdown; occurred between the years 2006 thru 2009. From January 2006 till December of 2007 the score varied between four and seven. In January of 2008 the score jumped to eight. Indicators, **PPI-A, CPI-U, USD/EUR, MM, OIL, Gold, Housing and UNEMP** indicated. With the current analysis **UNEMP** will have to be neglected, because it was below 6.5 % most of 2008. In February of 2008 **COMO** was added so the score was nine. The score varied between seven eight and nine till October 2008. At this point, included in my technical analysis will be market averages. The SP-500 began to collapse on October 10, 2007. A trend-line drawn from October 10, 2007 to December 13, 2007 was never breached; it was downhill all the way to March 9, 2009, the bottom of the SP-500 during that time period.

The Three Month Treasury Bill **3MTB** only indicated a problem in February and March of 2007. Then again economic condition did not exist where the **3MTB** would be useful. Consequently, I still feel that the **3MTB** should be kept as an indicator. There are two reasons it represents a competing investment to the stock market. Also, it is an interest rate that the FED controls. This was a complex period in the US economy.

It seems that since the beginning of time, Gold has been viewed as an inflation hedge. During periods of inflation and uncertainty, investors invest in gold. Almost all of 2006 to 2011 the gold indicator indicated a problem. There were four sporadic months that the gold indicator did not indicate a problem. There was one in December of 2008 and three in early 2009.

The above discussion highlights that investment decisions are not guided by axioms related to an exact science. Indicators, similar to investing, are a **current activity**. An investor must be alert to the possibility that some action by any source may render a particular indicator; dominant or not useful.

An example may illustrate my point. Let us assume that after draining mid-America for thousands of years; a dome of oil is discovered under the Mississippi river. Furthermore, the discovery resulted in a find that is the largest oil discovery in history and it is ten times larger than the Saudi Arabian oil discovery. The oil indicator is not necessary.

EFFECT OF FOREIGN ECONOMIES

For the years 2011 to 2012, the turmoil in a number of foreign economies is affecting markets in the United States. The assessment of the numerous foreign economies is beyond the scope of this layman investor. The approach that this layman investor is going to rely on is stock technical analysis as described above.

NO	INDICATOR	WEB SITE
1	PPI	bls.gov/xg_shells/ro2xgppihistall.htm
2	CPI-U	bls.gov/cpi/
3	USD/EUR	usforex.com/forex-tools/my-fx-dashboard
4	COMMODITY	indexmundi.com/commodities/?commodity=industrial-inputs-price-index&months=300
5	3MTB	treasury.gov/resource-center/data-chart-center/interest-rates/Pages/TextView.aspx?data=yield
6(a)	H6	federalreserve.gov/releases/H6/about.htm
6(b)	H3	federalreserve.gov/releases/h3/current/h3.htm
7	DIVISIA M4	centerforfinancialstability.org/amfm_data.php
8	GOLD	chart service
9	OIL	indexmundi.com/commodities/?commodity=crude-oil-west-texas-intermediate&months=300
10	Housing	census.gov/construction/nrc/
11	P/E	multpl.com/
12	DIVIDEND	multpl.com/s-p-500-dividend-yield/
13	unemployment	bls.gov/timeseries/LNS14000000

NOTE: Preceding all addresses is   http://www.

Figure 5-1

A picture is worth eight hundred words and two hundred tea leaves.

CHAPTER 6

GRAPHIC AND TECHNICAL ANALYSIS & FINAL COMMENTS

As stated in Chapter 5 the explanation of the process is more complex than the procedure. I have a three ring binder with thirteen dividers. In between the dividers are data sheets. Once a month I go on line and at each specific web site, I gather the data. The data is then inputted into each sheet of the spreadsheet program. At that point an investor can evaluate the results. I feel that the process is relatively simple.

Rather than just having discrete indicators; I feel that graphic analysis and technical analysis adds useful features to the procedure. Since data was already available in each specific indicator sheet, I decided to plot the data. Also, technical analysis of the stock market averages and individual stocks is performed with Worden Brothers TC-2000 ®.

This analysis is not a judgment of the FED's action; it is a mathematical review of the results. As part of my analysis I wrote a program where I kept the monthly year over year growth in money supply, a constant percentage. It is a laborious process and once this is accomplished, a graph of the monthly percentage year over year growth in money supply is graphically a flat line.

Also, I analyzed the **monthly** **year** over **year** percentage growth of two money supplies, **M2** and **DIVISIA M4** for the period January 2006 thru July of 2013. It was very informative; they both were not flat lines. To me, this indicates either a planned change of money supply growth, or an imperfection in the control of money supply growth. The money supply with the largest variation was Divisia M4. The data for both money supplies is depicted in the Figure 6-1.

OBSERVATION OF THE DATA FROM 2005 TO 2013

The **MM** indicator indicated in 2005, 2006, 2007, and most all of 2008. To this layman, it indicates excessive money supply growth during those years.

Now the question is: **What money supply measure indicates excessive money supply growth?**

When one observes the monthly plots of both M2 and Divisa M4, from January 2005 on, it seems that M2 is more linear than Divisia M4. The upward slope of Divisa M4 is greater than M2 till January of 2009. Divisa M4 then has a negative slope till April 2010. From then on, Divisa M4 seems to have less of an upward slope than M2. This correlates with the monthly percent year over year growth in both of these measures of money supply.

PERCENT MONTHLY YEAR OVER YEAR CHANGE IN MONEY SUPPLY

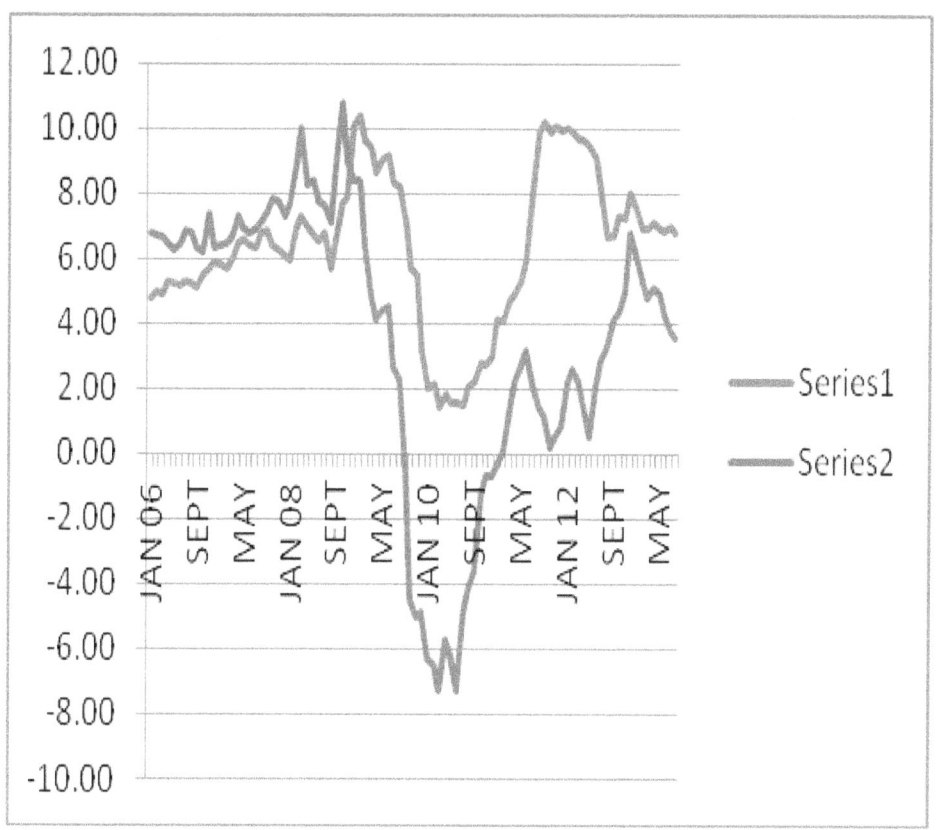

FIGURE 6-1

Series 1 is M2 upper curve right side.

Series 2 is Divisa M4 lower curve right side.

Since I have had no formal training in economics; in layman terms, it seems that excessive money supply growth became apparent, and the growth in money supply was contracted excessively. This was confirmed by the indicator **MSM**. From September of 2009 thru February of 2011 it indicated money supply contractions.

Also, debasing of the dollar was evident. The USD/EUR reached a value of 1.579 in March of 2008 and a value of 1.2748 in February of 2009.

The CPI-U went from plus 5.6% in July of 2008 to minus 2.1% in July of 2009.

The above values, confirm the dynamics in the money supply.

THE ECONOMY AND THE STOCK MARKET

Federal Reserve Chairman, Ben Bernanke has been attempting to right a collapsed housing market with a low interest rate policy. The housing market started to show some life; but has not fully recovered. Also, there seems to be some correlation between money supply and job growth. Figure 6-2 indicates as money supply is contracted unemployment increases (job loss) and conversely when money supply expands unemployment decreases (job increase). Also, as mention above, the money supply seems to be below a growth level.

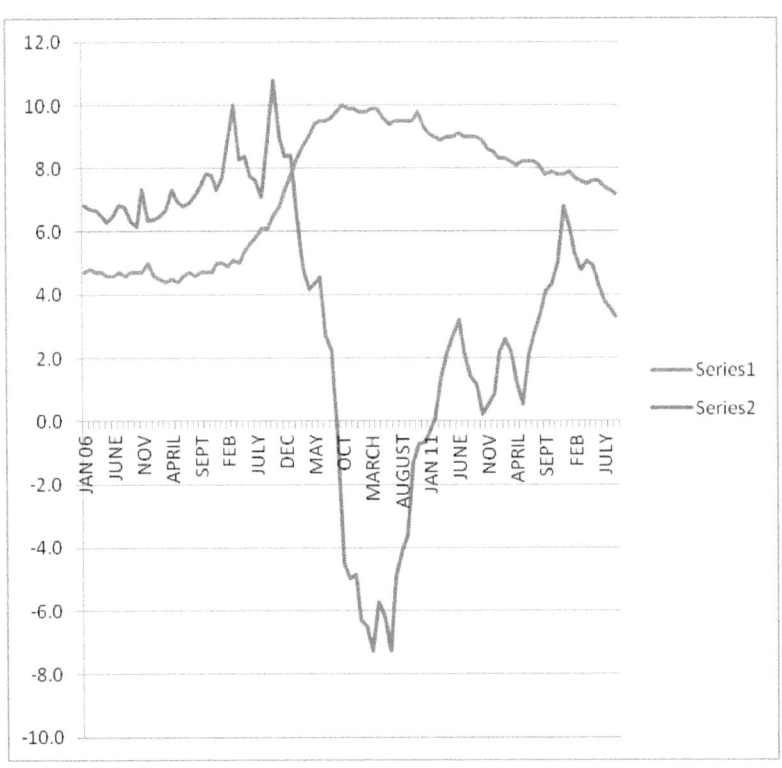

FIGURE 6-2

Series 1 is UNEMPLOYMENT upper line right side.

Series 2 is Divisa M4 lower line right side

It is interesting to note, that by viewing money supply and the USD/EUR ratio, one can deduce that to date, the sweet spot to invest in gold was, from 2006 thru 2011. Investment in gold is highly correlated with the FED's ability to prevent debasement of the dollar.

Low interest rates have made the stock market the only hope for added return. I am amazed by the action of the current stock market. Chairman Bernanke clearly states that he is going to continue Quantitative easing [print more money] and the stock market soars. I own a few stocks; but have an uneasy feeling.

An investor should carefully monitor Indicator #3 USD/EUR to determine whether the dollar is debased, causing commodity prices to soar; inflation.

Money, in a sense, is stored in banks. Clearly a great deal of money has been created by the FED. As previously mentioned I am not sufficiently schooled to know what it will take to get this money judiciously made available to the business community. An investor should be concerned if there is a continual lack of money for business creation. Secondly, will the money be released in a sense, in a flood, that will lead to inflation? A lack of attentive control should be a concern to an investor.

Indicators #2 CPI-U, #5 3MTB, and #6 MM should be closely monitored.

Have a good day! MSL

www.ingramcontent.com/pod-product-compliance
Lightning Source LLC
Chambersburg PA
CBHW081356170526
45166CB00010B/3109